My Journey As A Medium

Caroline Ann Coe

Copyright: Caroline Ann Coe 2016
ISBN: 978-1-326-89174-9

Introduction

I have been prompted for a long time to write. My story is slightly different. I am a Medium who just happens to have had a near death experience that has led me onto a journey I would never have anticipated.

This book shares a part of my life with you. It has been a journey that in a lot of ways is very similar to yours. Like you, I have experienced many difficult things in my life. Some I have shared here, the most relevant ones that make up my story, but others I have not for personal reasons.

I have talked about my younger years and the significance of people being in my life because they have all led me to exactly where I am today.
In looking back, I believe that my destiny was already set in stone. I was meant to become a medium.

I believe a lot of problems that we have today are the result of not feeling loved. I believe through different experiences we lose sight of who we really are, forgetting that we are unique, beautiful human beings. Throughout our lives, we have been shown and reminded of this in the people that we have met. We will see things in them we like but these parts of themselves that we recognise are aspects of ourselves. They have held up a mirror that we are reflected in. The timing of these moments are quite often amazing in their synchronicity. I know we are guided and looked after always by the spirit world.

I have shared just a few of my experiences when I have worked with the spirit world, how the evidence is given to me, how I work with the information and my communicators in the spirit world and how that information is passed on to the recipient. I have changed names and some finer details, such as venue and gender of people, for reasons of confidentiality.

I am not a writer but have always loved putting pen to paper. Neither am I the most organized of people so this has all been a bit hit and miss. I had a dream and was reminded by someone in the spirit world, "It's important to get going with your writing". So here it is.

My hope is that it helps you in some way. I hope that it brings forward good memories that come into your mind and from there enabling you to remember how much you are loved and how special you really are.

As I am writing my introduction, my book is being edited, proof read and prepared for publication I have thoughts and ideas tumbling through my head for more writing with a thumbs up from the spirit world x

                      Love

Caroline Ann Coe x

Love

We cannot touch it, we cannot bottle it, and we cannot see it.

"But we can see it we see in the eyes of a loved one. We see it the face of child. We see in the greatest and most precious moments of our lives. Weddings, births and the saddest of all deaths. We feel it in all of these things."

Ask someone who is suffering the loss of a loved one where they feel the pain? They will put their hands on their hearts.
Ask someone where they feel joy and they will put their hands on their hearts.
Ask someone where they feel sadness and they will put their hands on their hearts.

The heart is the seat of emotion, the golden bridge between the soul and the world. We see with our eyes, process with our minds but our hearts always, without a shadow of doubt, tell us the truth. The soul/heart heart/soul both are intertwined as is love.

We are all on the same journey to discover love because that is all that matters.
I do know that the bonds and ties of love, the connections of heart and soul can never ever be broken. Love lives on. It survives the death of our physical bodies. I know this with a certainty and confidence that cannot be shaken. I just know. How do I know this?

Chapter One

I came into the world in Germany at a military hospital in a place called Iserlohn on the 13th of September, 1960, weighing the same as a bag of sugar. My twin sister was a little bigger than me at 2 pound 6 ounces. We were born at around 26 weeks. I do not know the exact time. We were not expected to live. In those days, medical care wasn't anywhere near as it is today for pre-term babies. Our births were not registered until we were six months old.

My dad, James Tetlow, was a Lancashire man who joined the army from Newton Le Willows grammar school in the town of St. Helens in Merseyside. He was 15. All my family on my dad's side are from Lancashire.

Mum and Dad met in Malaya, where my mum's dad Donald Brant (Grandad Don) was also serving in the army. He was with the engineers and Dad was with the Queen Lancashire Regiment. My mum's mum was Theresa Elizabeth Brant. I don't know a lot about her life but her mother was Indian and worked as a school teacher in India where she met and married my great grandad who was also with the British army. Although I don't know much about them I do believe my great grandad was an Irishman.

My mum and dad got married in Malaya. They married in the local Catholic church and had their wedding reception in Raffles which was and is today, a very exclusive place. He was ten years older than Mum. She was just 18 years old when they married. We lived in Germany for the first couple of years in an army quarter.

I have no recollection of this time, but pictures bring back certain memories. The double buggy my sister and I shared and our sun hats. I am not sure why I remember those. There was a part of our lives that was not the norm. Mum was ill and had kidney disease. It was advised by the doctors that she did not have children as her kidneys would not cope. But she did and became pregnant with not just one baby but two: my sister and me.

I think all three of us struggled to live during this period. My sister and myself in the womb and mum, who had pre-eclampsia. Our arrival into the world was a miracle and the fact we both survived was a bigger one.

From Germany, we moved to Barnard Castle in County Durham where we lived in an army quarter. Army quarters were all very similar, as they are today, and it's amazing to look at the pictures as there are hardly any cars as we would see today. The streets look unusually large, wide, empty and uncluttered.

Traditional picket fences, neat square gardens and tidy borders created the entrance from a little wooden gate that attached itself comfortably to the path leading up to the front door that sat perfectly on a stone step that was quite often painted in a maroon colour. There were no plastic windows back then and no double glazing. All the windows were wood, as was the front door. Perhaps that is one reason why winters felt like winters indoors as well as out in those days.

Mum was very ill during this period but she lived for another three years. A month after our third birthday in November 1963, she died. It was very quick. She died very suddenly and unexpectedly at home with my dad and my aunty Joan beside her.

This is how we came into the world. We made it. I feel as if our mum's gift to us was life. Against all the odds we both survived. I always felt there was a reason why I survived. I didn't know why but what I did know was that I would do something out of the ordinary with my life. I had no idea what it was for a number of years.

Chapter Two

Stop daydreaming! Wake up! Dilly daydream that was my name. I remember my childhood as being one where I was crippled with shyness. I was called shy, anti-social but I wasn't any of these things. I realize now I was highly, highly sensitive.
I didn't like being around a lot of people (I am not very comfortable with this today). I ran a mile when I was confronted with very noisy outgoing people (I would do this today if I could). I loved quietness. I did not like arguing or discord (I don't today) and I always felt as if I never fit in. I was an introvert. I was the leader of the sheep, never the leader and I realize now I was naturally drawn to people who were like me because they understood.

I believe this is very common amongst sensitives and is now understood far more than it was years ago. Does it sound familiar?

My introduction to the Spirit world started, I recall, when I was three years old and my mum died. This was a tragedy not only for my sister and me but one that had far reaching ripples, not only through my childhood years but into my adult life as well. It has also shaped my life or my life has been shaped around it. Did I become a medium because of this very significant event in my childhood or was there a bigger plan? Was this meant to happen to lead me onto to a path of discovery about what death and love are?

I had another challenge. Not only had we lost our mum tragically to kidney disease that today could have been cured, I had a twin sister. We were and are to this day very different. Polar opposites. She made up for my quietness by being very noisy, naughty and outgoing. I made up for her noisiness by being ultra-quiet, sensitive and meek. Together we made a perfect match. If all the ingredients were mixed together. But it was difficult to mix them up. She did everything to gain attention and I did everything to try and avoid it.

We went to live with my grandmother Terry and granddad Don, my mums' parents. My dad was in the army and did not have time to take care of two lively three year olds.

It was during this period I had my first experience of what I call the spirit world. I had seen my mum and she appeared in a long flowing gown. I sat with my aunty Hilary, my dads' sister, one day and said "Mummy has got a dress like that". She had a dressing gown on. I saw her. I remember her face and shock to this day. But I also knew that my mum was real and there was something else.

My sister also had her own experience. We were four years old and living in a very old dorma bungalow that was surrounded by huge Hydrangeas that felt as if they had been there forever. They merged into the brickwork and the soul of this beautiful chocolate box 1960's bungalow with its smiling bay windows.

She used to carry a matchbox around in her pocket. It went everywhere with her. I asked her one day what she had in the match box "Look" she said. I looked and looked but all I could see was a piece of tissue paper. "Can you see her?" Nope, I tried and tried to see something else in that box but couldn't "It's Tinkerbell". She then began to take her out of the box and hold her very gently in her hand. "Look" but I still could not see her. I believe it was a 'fairy' as my sister used to call

her, or a nature spirit. I believed she was there but I also believe she was my sisters' companion to help her through her childhood years.
We have talked about it recently and 'Tinkerbell' stayed with her until she was about six. She still remembers her very clearly. I never doubted she was there and slept in that match box but was always puzzled and not a little bit miffed as to why I couldn't see her.

How many of you had a special friend in your childhood?

The grieving around his time could be felt and being very sensitive I felt it. What I also felt with my sensitivity was the love. Love for my sister and me. A love that has lived in my heart through this experience. The death of my mum had been planted in my soul to stay there forever.

Throughout my years, it has stayed with me. I was lucky I knew what love was. I have always felt and knew we were loved by Grandmas, Granddads, Aunties and uncles. I thank them for that because as life became more difficult I always knew I was loved even though we had lost our mum. So, I experienced and felt love. l felt the grief and sadness and experienced this and I also learnt and felt and saw the spirit world all in three short years.

As I look back to this early time of my life, I realize I could sense a gentle vibration around me. I always had a knowing of something around me and I always knew I would be protected by unseen forces. I also realized the power then and now of love. It is the greatest force that we can ever experience.
How many of you were loved unconditionally if only by one person in your childhood?

Chapter Three

They say that this Psychic gift runs in families. My grandmother Terry was a medium. She was very dark haired, skinned and beautiful. She was also very wide and very, very short at 4 foot 11. She loved bright beads, big rings and silk scarves. She wore kaftans to hide her size and she had a huge heart.

After our mum died she sat with us both and talked about guardian angels. We were three years old. This is what she said.
"We all have a guardian angel. Someone who takes care of us all through our life. They never leave us and if you are ever worried about anything just ask and they will be right beside you."
My future had been sealed. I believed every word she said. I felt it. And I knew she was right because I knew that something else existed.
I did not know she was a medium until she had passed into the spirit world.

So, we continued to grow up my sister and me. I seemed to become quieter and she seemed to become increasingly noisy. My sister, as I have already mentioned, was very different from me she was like my grandmother: outgoing, fearless, and gregarious and always getting into trouble.

She ate snails, played with worms and got mucky in the space of seconds. She stole my food when I wasn't looking, my hat when it was hot and once, I believe, stuck postage stamps all over the wall. She said everything very loudly and I sulked. My grandmother understood her. They were like peas in a pod, although I'm not sure about grandma eating snails or playing with worms though I expect she was too old! This is how they seemed to my quiet world.

I hated getting dirty, was scared of worms and snails (never mind eating them). I was scared of falling over and looked as if I had just walked out of the washing machine and off the ironing board (without trying). I was also labelled as 'the pretty one'. My sister was the 'tomboy'.

There were two people in my life at this time that I loved very much and completely understood my quiet ways. They were my two granddads. Granddad Don that I lived with, even though I used to cry when he made me eat fried bread. I hated it and I thought it was wrong to make someone eat something they didn't like. My sensitivity gave me a heightened sense of what was right and wrong even at a young age.

I though, was his favourite and like me he was quiet. I realize now our energies were similar. He was an army man as well and to my littleness at the time he seemed like a giant. I saw him years later before he passed and he looked tiny to how I remembered him. He had a look for many different things and you knew what the look meant. He didn't need to speak, you just knew. He walked into a room and you knew he had made an entrance, it was just the way he was.

He was a gentleman, fair, honest, strict and kind with a roaring sense of humour and a laugh to match. He loved pork pies (and the jelly). I used to watch him eat them and it made me feel sick. He didn't however, make me eat them. Funny what you remember. I don't eat pork pies today but every time I see one I think of him.
My other granddad, my dads' dad, was Granddad Jim. I didn't see a lot of him but I loved him very much. He

again was an Army man and rose to the rank of Major. I only ever remember him having one leg. I thought he had lost his leg due to shrapnel in the first world war but it wasn't, he had Diabetes.

The only thing I knew about Diabetes then was that you could buy sweets in a tin with no sugar in them. He had them on the table beside his chair. We used to buy him them. They were always coated in white floury stuff. He could never open the tin with his arthritic fingers but neither could I with my little ones.

He always smelt of cabbage (I didn't understand this until years later when I did my nurse training). I felt sorry for him then and my heart went out to every old man I nursed who had that smell because I understood.
He smoked a pipe. I used to watch with fascination as he lit his pipe and made circles with smoke that rose to the ceiling and then disappeared into nothingness. With my first pocket money from a paper-round I bought him a new pipe.

He was surrounded by bits and pieces from his army years. He was the commandant of the army camp in County Durham called Harporley and was surrounded by things the prisoners had given him. A painting from an Italian man hung on the wall above the china cupboard. A table made out of match sticks. I loved the intricacy of that table it was varnished and very beautiful. I remember thinking "prisoners are very clever" and they must have liked him very much. He always said treat people how you want to be treated. Harporley camp exists today and granddad is mentioned as running the camp, Major James Tetlow.

I have always had an interest in the Second World War. Granddad was evacuated from Dunkirk before the proper invasion as a part of the exhibitionary force. If he hadn't I wouldn't be here. Something had for some time always bothered me. I had read about the POW camps in Germany and Japan since and always had this little niggling thought; were the camps here as great as Granddad said? The beautiful objects he was surrounded by that were created for him by the Italian prisoners; the little table made from wood with inlaid wooden patterns, the painting hanging on the wall above the ticking clock on the sideboard confirmed this but still.

We have recently been to Spain on holiday, sitting at the breakfast table when all of a sudden, I felt granddad beside me. "Granddads here Peter" I said to my husband. There was no response from him at all for at least five seconds and then he said "Why is he here?"
"I don't know." I didn't know but I was curious. The answer as to why came later on at dinner time.

We sat by a lovely couple from Liverpool as we were waiting to go for dinner and for some reason she started to tell us about her dad. "He was in Stalag concentration camp you know." The film Great Escape was Stalag. I was fascinated. "Was he a part of the escape?"
"No but he used to collect the dirt as it was being dug out and spread it around the camp. He never spoke about it very much."
"My granddad was commandant at a camp in County Durham." She had seen what her dad had been through in a POW CAMP and just looked at me and pulled a face (not a happy one).

Peter and myself then had a conversation. He told me about the Italians in the war and how they were more than happy to be caught by the British and sent over here as life in a camp here was a thousand times better than that in occupied Europe. I recalled Granddad telling me that in that moment and my queries about the Harporly camp were resolved.

This was not the only experience I had on this holiday. I believe the first experience on the journey was a taste of what was to come. We went on a bus to Spain as Peter has a fear of flying. We travelled through France. I looked up and saw a sign for the town of Ypres. I realized I had read books and that this was the town. In world war one there was a battle called the "battle of Ypres" As I was thinking this all of a sudden I saw a solider dressed in all his army gear, his tin hat, rifle etc. run down the middle of the bus as he was in a huge hurry to get somewhere. I heard the name George and have just been told his surname was Jones.

We will always be given answers to questions we have but we have to be open to the message.

I got my interest in people from this chapter in my life and later on my love of psychology because I wanted to understand, and because of granddad Jim.
He had long fingers like me and thin legs. Both his parents died when he was a boy and he was sent away to America for a while to live with relatives. He didn't have to say anything he just got it, he understood because he had experienced the same thing. I think that is what empathy is called, the ability to put your self in another's shoes and to understand.

Have you ever experienced the ability to "understand" someone because of a shared experience you have been through?

I used to write his letters for him to a daughter he had who lived in Cornwall (with him telling me what to write) and read the papers to him as he was nearly blind. A common comment "What a load of rubbish! Things weren't like that when I was a boy!" Sound familiar? He always used to say being a Lancashire man "there is nowt as funny as folk." I have remembered that phrase many times during my life.

I wrote a story about him when I was in my first year at secondary school and I won! It was about the wisdom of his wrinkles and how each wrinkle on his face told a story about his life. I was eleven.

I loved my Granddad even though he smelt of cabbage. He used to say to my sister all of the time, "If I had another leg!" She never loved him as I did and our memories of him are very, very different.

Do you have someone in your life that was completely inspiring only you didn't realize until you grew up just how much?

Granddad Jim and nana lived at 439 Wargrave Road. The house sat at the end of a long terrace of red brick, bay fronted houses with small front gardens and paved paths leading up to a big front door, stepping into a large hall with a mosaic tiled floor and very steep stairs in front. It was the "best" entrance and to my knowledge we never used it apart from the postman who put the letters through the outer door that always stuck and rattled when nana picked up the post.

We always went around the side of the house and went in through the gate that was snuggled perfectly within the high brick wall that enveloped the rose filled back garden with its small lawn that was cut with a little push lawn mower. The path from the gate to the back door was made of old slate and arranged into a herringbone pattern that had sunk in places but it was still very pretty. It had an old loo at the bottom that hadn't been used for many years (before my time) with a big white door with flaking paint and a rusty old key that hadn't been turned for sometime. It was out of bounds. But I didn't like it anyway, it was full of spiders and smelt of wee and must.

The house backed onto a race track. The Vulcan factory down the street originally made huge locomotives that were made for other countries in the world, particularly India, who did not have the capabilities to build their own. The huge factory has sadly been completely demolished and its place today stands a new housing estate. Next to the factory was a village called the Vulcan village was built to house all the workers. I knew that the people that lived there were poor and sensed that many people lived in each house. I never liked driving though it because it always seemed very dark and felt very heavy.

I also knew how lucky we were. The Vulcan village built for the factory workers still exists today and looks identical, as does the Vulcan pub.

We slept in the massive front bedroom with its ceiling to floor double sash windows that let in everything from wind, noise and moonlight. The wallpaper was blue and white and had cherubs on it. I used to stare at that wallpaper for ages when I was scared at night in the darkness of that huge cavernous room praying not to see anything in the dark corners. The bed was big and very high and the room was cold. With layers and layers of blankets it was best to stay in one spot and not move because it was only that spot that kept warm. My nanny used to appear sometimes on scary nights and hug us until we fell asleep.

Our Mum's memory was also kept alive in that room in a box underneath the bed. It was full of letters, postcards, and cards from mum to dad when they were away from each other. My sister and I used to get it out and read all the things in it. I felt my mum in those letters, in the words, between the lines, the commas like breaths and the full stops like pauses. I felt her energy. I can read a book today and I feel as if I know the author, not just because of the content of a book but because of the energy behind it. I felt my mum within and around those letters.

My Nan was a knitter. I used to hold her hanks of wool while she made them up into a ball to knit. I have never seen anyone knit like her since or ever likely to. Like the speed of lightening and she could multitask while doing it. She knitted my sister and me matching jumpers. I though, was at an age when I really did not want to dress or look like my sister or wear knitted jumpers, but we wore them anyway and have photos in our handmade outfits. It was a house of learning, calm, pipe smoke, books, old things, ticking clocks, no fridges or hot running water and love.

We have all had a place like this in our childhoods.

My sister's memories are different. Although it was a place she liked to go, she did not have the same relationship with Grandad Jim.
We had a chat very recently, she started to talk about the house. She said "Do you remember the bathroom?"
"Yes, it was huge"
"Do you remember the wall paper?"
"No"
"It was covered in fish. The whole room was covered in it." That was her memory. My memory of the room is

that we never had a bath because it took too long to fill up. I have no recollection of the wallpaper.
I remembered the wall paper in the huge bedroom. As I mentioned previously, it was covered in blue cherubs because I spent ages next to it and staring at it. And she remembers the wall paper in the bathroom.

Perhaps interestingly as siblings, we have different memories for different reasons. Different things stand out. Even now I love wall paper and material with cherubs on it and she has fish in her bathroom.

I love Victorian fireplaces, the little ones in bedrooms, roses, walled gardens and slate paving. The smell of pipes, clocks ticking, the smell of old books and being warm. I am fascinated by the past, the Victorian times, and would rather buy an old piece of furniture than a new one because it has history and a story to tell just like Nana and Grandad's house. My sister does not like any of those things. But she is a brilliant knitter, just like nan.

What positive memories do you have of things in your childhood that you love now?

Chapter Four

After my mum died when we were three we went to live with Granddad Don and Grandma Terry. My dad used to visit us. My sister and me used to sleep in a big double bed. I don't remember her in it. Maybe the bed was very, very big. It had to be otherwise I'd have known. I always remember him reading Winnie the Pooh as a bedtime story. I used to fall asleep and wake up in the morning and he would be gone. I loved Winnie the Pooh then and I have loved Winnie the Pooh ever since. I love the simplicity and wisdom of the words.

My grandmother was a catholic until her first divorce after the church disowned her. I always believed in a God, Jesus, what ever you want to call it and used to say my prayers before I went to bed at night. I used to talk to my mum. I had a teddy bear. It was bought from Germany when we were born. I still have it today. His nose has a bald patch where I used to rub it and his hand is worn where I held it. He went everywhere with me, as did our dog Shep. He was a cross border collie and he was my companion.

We continued to live with my Granddad Don and Granny Terry. My mum was very much alive for all of us at this time in conversations, in things we did, in memories shared by my Nana and Granddad.
I also, at this time, still felt the presence of the spirit world or the energy of something else around me. It was there continuously and gave me something extra. This was also kept alive by my granny who believed in God, the spirit world. She spoke about angels and as I think of her at that time I realize her energy was one of love. She oozed it. She had a very big heart as well as a very big personality.

She called me Bambi. It was a very apt name as I also looked like a baby deer with huge brown eyes and a delicate nature.

We were very privileged. Dad had been promoted within the officer ranks. We lived in a huge house in Malta on a hill with a veranda that went all around it overlooking Valetta bay. My sister was not happy and neither was our new stepmother. My sister was very close to my grandmother and my grandmother and step mum disliked each other instantly (dislike I believe is a very mild word to use).

I believe with adult eyes that they were both jealous of each other. The memory of my mum lived on in my sister and me and my grandmother being psychic herself must have had an inkling of how things were about to unravel. But my dad wanted us with him. The decision was made.

I continued to be my quiet self and my sister now was not only being outgoing but also began to be naughty. It was a difficult time for her and all of us, a time of adjustment to a new life. I loved colours, crayoning, school, music and I was learning to play the recorder.

We had a young girl called Maria who used to come and clean our hall floor (I am sure she cleaned other places as well but I only remember the hall). It was a vast marble floor laid out in a diamond pattern of pale, large shiny marble floor tiles. She used to wash it in huge figures of eight, twice with soap suds and then with a wet mop. I was fascinated.

I have never been able to wash the floor like that (my floors have always been considerably smaller) or seen soap suds like it. Every time I wash a floor I think of Maria.

I really liked Maria. She couldn't speak much English but she was a very good nodder and smiled a lot. I used to sit on the floor and watch her. I realize now I liked her energy. I understood her and she understood me. She was also a catholic and perhaps I sensed her belief like mine and it made me feel comfortable. She was also my equal because of her energy and nature.

My childhood was like that one big feeling of who I did and did not feel comfortable with. I am still like that today.

The Rickshaw man.
He used to take us into Valletta in his old battered Rickshaw. One day the wheel fell off. We were all ok and it is from this particular day that I have my memories of him. He had no teeth and he looked like a battered old leather suitcase of at least 150 years old. He was wrinkled by the sun and by cigarettes, he had one permanently hanging out of his mouth which probably helped with the wrinkles. He had the most amazing sparkle in his eyes and the kindest nature. That is why I liked him.

The Goat lady
You could hear her coming, the tinkling of bells that got louder and louder and the sound of a Maltese lady calling to the goats as if they were her friends. She looked old (perhaps older than she was), she wore a headscarf and apron that she collected mushrooms in that grew beyond our sight. She wore a dress underneath her pinny and had vast bosoms and legs to match at the end of which she wore boots and ankle socks.

She used to dip her old, dirty, well worn work hands into the pocket in her pinny and pull out a handful of mushrooms that were already wrapped in a handkerchief for us. She was a very simple native Maltese lady and she spoke no English. I liked her.

Two more of those beautiful souls I have never forgotten, and as I write I sense the old woman with me. She says "Bambino".

I knew these people, they taught me, looking back, at the beauty and simplicity of the human soul.
I continued to be quiet and was painfully shy but I was happy and content in my own little world.   So, life continued. I loved my school in Malta, loved learning, music, art/colours and continued to connect with certain people, mostly what we would call in my adult life the poor and under privileged, but to me they were rich in something that I sensed but couldn't be put into words.

I recently read a quote that perhaps sums this up "Wealth cannot be counted by material possessions".

Do you have someone in your childhood that was not family that you met briefly and really felt at one with who you have never forgotten?

My dad asked the army P.T. instructor to teach us to swim in a Lido. Looking back, I really don't know what possessed him. A lido was a platform in the sea that smelt of old rubber tyres or whatever it was made of and always moved in the opposite direction that you wanted it to when you tried to climb on to it. This was difficult because the water was beyond standing depth.

My sister refused point blank to get in the water because someone told her there were   shark nets and she told my dad she was not going back. She did not want to be eaten by sharks.

I had a quiet, steely determination to achieve and beat any obstacle that was put in front of me. I learnt to swim and was luckily not eaten by or did I ever see a shark.
We both looked forward to letters from our granny Terry. She would send pictures of kangaroos and koala bears on postcards that looked as if they were real. They moved, hopped and jumped when you wiggled the card. Her letters were full of news, concern and love. They arrived regularly, always with a small gift (usually from Hong Kong) that was sparkly and pretty. She sent us a couple of matching outfits. I have a photograph of us standing outside our house in Malta. My husband says we look like the Von Trapps.

From Australia, my nanny Terry and grandad Don moved to Papau New Guinea where grandad became head of the colonial police force. Their letters were now not only full of love and news, but also full of rude phrases (to two eight year olds) in pigeon English. Funny but beautiful and interesting descriptions of how the native tribes lived, mostly on houses with stilts because of the snakes, spiders and other creepy crawlies that would have been desperate to bite anything human. It was a culture that was very underdeveloped, as were the people at that time.

This job would have suited grandad Don perfectly with his fair, respectful, gentlemanly and straight forward approach to life. I again had a message from him in 2015 at the AFC college, "Who knows a policeman and a grandad in the spirit world?" Me.

We had a family day on Sunday in the large front room with its huge ceiling fans and polished floor. The large wooden painted shutters with huge slats on the tall numerous windows were folded across to keep the daytime sun out. My sister and I sat on the polished wooden parquet floor with our legs crossed, its tales of years gone by in the scratches and grooves told by the feet and furniture that had been moved across and sat on it, perhaps making new memories in the marks we made.

We all played Monopoly. These always felt like special times. My dad taught me how to count, add and subtract with monopoly money without me being aware of it by being my assistant banker. I can add up very quickly today. I quite often won at games even if I didn't know the game very well, and still do much to everyone's annoyance. I guess you could call it intuition. I had a feel for the right moves.

We all have these gems of memories tucked away of special moments in our lives.

Chapter Five

I had out of body experiences as a child. It is only recently (since writing this book) that I have been reminded of these in a dream. I do now remember these quite clearly. I felt as if I were flying above the trees, up, up and away the sense of freedom was amazing. I knew no one could reach me. I had dreams at this time of people running after me and I could run and lift myself off the ground so that I was flying above them. I recall going to different places but not too far as I thought I might not be able to get back.

I have skipped some of my formative years as they would probably appear quite boring. I don't recall anything very spiritual happening. I think it was a time when I was caught up in the normal day to day growing up stuff and worrying about my sister who now wore Doc Martins, long skirts and had friends who had bikes and wore leather jackets. She had a nose stud. She would fight at school (my step mother was horrified, girls don't fight). We had different friends. Nothing wrong with any of that just to my still sensitive world her world seemed a bit harsh. We were still complete opposites.

One thing I am really pleased about to this day is that we were both educated in Catholic Schools. Our mum was a catholic and this was her wish. Dad left the army in 1975 and we ended up settling in Manchester. We moved from Catterick in North Yorkshire from the comfort and security of an Army school where the kids were the same, spoke the same with no regional accent and had all travelled. It felt like we had gone to Mars (from Venus).

But we were closer in miles to Granddad and nana from 439 Wargrave road and it is from this period where I have some lovely memories.

From our Catholic school at the age of about 12, we were invited to go and see the nuns. I always wanted to be a nun as a child. I have a nun as a guide. I do not know where this place was or the nuns, only the experience remains.
They sat in their habits behind glass windows. I don't know why. I think they were quite safe. We could talk to them. I don't recall what I said to Mother Teresa or she said to me (I Don't think that was her name but they all seemed to be called Teresa, Bernadette, Mary, Catherine etc. after the saints). But afterwards I went and sat in the church that was attached to the nunnery.

In that time and place on a very simple uncomfortable wooden bench with its shelf holding a single mass book, a cushion to kneel on surrounded by the smell of incense, the light of burning candles, the peace and the sound of a young choir I felt an energy. It was the most powerful loving gentle thing I have ever felt and I knew it was God/spiritual whatever you want to call it.
It awoke in me the memory of the energy that I was surrounded by as a child, I recognised it. I have never forgotten it. I have been surrounded by it ever since.
Funnily enough, I wrote a poem recently, about love for my daughters wedding and it starts, "In this place, (church) in this moment, in this second of time".

All my experiences previously of the people I connected with as a seven year old; Maria, The Goat lady, the Rickshaw man. I had seen even at the age of seven, the soul within the man. These people were so closely connected to themselves created by their simple lives and their beliefs in something greater. As an adult I now recognised what I had seen. I have seen it since in hospices where I have worked as an adult, in a few rare and truly spiritual people I have met along my pathway as a medium and it is beautiful. It is a just being. A letting go of ego and the material world into the spiritual without even knowing it. This is what these people showed me at a difficult transition in my childhood and I will be forever grateful to them and to those guardian angles that my nana talked about. They showed me the essence of who they are which is love.

I feel as if here I would like to mention Paul. Paul went to the same Catholic school as me and he was a friend of my sisters (but I liked him). He was gentle but most of all he was quiet and shy like me. I understood him. He wanted me to be his girlfriend but I just liked him. I knew him for a few years from the age of 15-17 when I left home and did my nurse training.

I went home one weekend from the hospital. My sister said "Paul has died in an accident". He was on his beloved bike; he saved years for it by working on his auntie's farm. He bought his bike when I had left home. He died immediately. The impact this had on me was very significant. I wondered about the grief his parents were feeling, his sister, his best friend Stuart, but I knew he was ok. Because I dreamt about him.

I have since had messages from him from mediums. The most significant one at the Arthur Findlay College in 2015. I know it is him, blonde hair, bike and he always says the same thing. Thank you for my friendship. I helped him believe in himself because he was like me.

I think we all meet people like us that we help without knowing it.

Amanda was a friend at the catholic school we went to. I am mentioning her because of the part she has played in my life up until today. She was tall, very attractive and had a great personality. She always looked nice without being too fashionable. She was also a quarter Jewish. Her mum was from Israel. She had a traditional Jewish shaped nose. She used to go away to Israel with her mum, dad and sister once a year. We worked at the same place when we left school but in separate offices in an Electro motor company just outside Manchester. It took two bus rides to get there and back. I liked her, she was different and we stayed friends for many years. I realise now why I liked her. Her family (some of them) had escaped the Nazi regime. She had a depth and maturity that not many people of our age had. I believe this was due in part to her family history.

Chapter Six

My first job was a paper round that my sister and I shared. She did the early morning round, I couldn't get out of bed (nothing has changed!) and I did the evening round. Sundays, we shared. A nightmare. The papers were huge because of the supplements and the letter boxes were never big enough. The bag was heavy and some of the littlest dogs were ferocious. Complaints were frequent at the beginning as the wrong paper or half a paper or a magazine without the paper went in the wrong box, in the wrong combination or not at all. But it worked out in the end. You learnt whose grass you could walk across, where the meanest dogs (and their owners) were located and how to avoid them. The smallest letter boxes, the biggest letter boxes and houses with porches that you could throw them in if they had a dog. I didn't have any spiritual experiences during this period but I did write another story entitled "My paper round" and it won an award.

In my first grown up job I worked in an office (I wasn't very good at it) and was always getting into trouble for not adding something up from the thousands of numbers to be imputed on the machine. I lost the will after a while, it was so boring. It was a purchase office so there were lots of pieces of paper. I don't recall what I did with them apart from put them in some sort of order. There was an eclectic mix of people in my particular office.

Susie, who was also an office junior until I arrived, was very bubbly and smiley and was at least four foot with, I seem to remember, tiny hairy hands and a black moustache. She sat by me.

Ingrid was from Holland and I asked her once how long she had lived in Manchester. She said since the 2nd world war and kept saying it was terrible, terrible. She didn't say anything else. She didn't want to talk about it and I didn't ask. She was a lovely gentle person and was quite elderly. She later on inspired me to find out what was so terrible.

Roy (the boy) was trained as a podiatrist (I didn't get how you can go from working with peoples' feet to paper). He was a bit creepy to my young self and he picked his nose, which was the reason I gave for leaving. He did though, give me a lovely reference but did whisper in my ear "Don't kill anyone" when I left to do my nurse training.

Our manger was called Mr Smart. Everybody moaned about him and said how miserable he was. I liked him. I sensed something really sad about him and later found out his wife had died.

I moved from the office and worked across the way in wages. I had an inbuilt knowing of how to sort the wages problems out due to those games of Monopoly back in Malta. I quite enjoyed it. I was also sent into Manchester once a week on a Wednesday to the bank. I can't remember what I did in the bank but I enjoyed the bus ride and I got expenses.

Amanda and I went to college to do typing. I hated it. It was the second most boring thing. I was a hopeless typist and was asked to type letters for the new boss of the cost office (my third move) but they always came back. Pitman's shorthand. I didn't get it at all; squiggles, line, dots, upside down, back to front. I am sure it would have been better to write in my own short hand that I could understand and then translate. I think my boss must have been tearing his hair out, although he didn't have much maybe that was the reason. Tippex was a wonderful thing.

I decided after not very long I really did not want to be in an offce surrounded by four walls with "grown up" mature people who picked their nose for the rest of my life. And I wasn't very good at it anyway and it wasn't very good with me. I now do office work!

Nursing. The adventure begins. I had been interviewed and accepted at the Robert Jones and Agnus Hunt Orthopaedic Hospital.

We had previously moved from Venus to Mars (Richmond army to Manchester in 1975). This time it was like moving from Mars to the moon, it was so quiet. I lived in the nursing home and had my room and lodgings deducted from my wages. I was still shy and my first ward was a young male orthopaedic ward in the form of a barrack hut. It was impossible to get from one end to the other without walking down the middle of the ward to be given marks out of ten. Being young and bed bound they had nothing else to do (I got a ten!).

I enjoyed it but was homesick for the first few months. I missed Manchester and its buzz. But I made friends with people there who I have kept in contact with.

I believe I was still at an age where I was experiencing life, but the spiritual side surfaced or special moments reminded me of my spiritual side during this period. Most of these moments I have never forgotten.

The sister on the ward asked me if I would sit with an old lady that was dying, it was my second ward, a geriatric ward. She was slowly slipping away and she had few family. I held her hand. It wasn't awful or horrible and I felt it was a privilege to sit with her.

I noticed on her bedside locker there was a little vase of lily of the valley. They were so pretty (I have loved them ever since). The sister of the ward had put them there. They were a sign of new beginnings for this lady as she passed. We had to wash and bathe her afterwards, comb her hair, put her teeth in and do other things that weren't so pleasant. She wasn't there, just the shell that had housed her body. "Remember it is the last thing you do for someone" said the sister. What a lovely lady she was, she had so much respect for all the elderly people she cared for. After that I did this job many times. I always said a quiet prayer that the person's soul would find heaven easily.

Miss Jones was our head tutor. She was thin and tall, wore plaid skirts, brown tights and flat lace up shoes. She had a hooked nose and had the wisest eyes behind her glasses (if you looked hard enough) you can imagine. She was the most knowledgeable person I have ever met.

I loved her physiology and anatomy classes, she was an inspiration. I found the human body absolutely fascinating. Everything was connected and I knew that the powers that are the creator in that moment existed without a shadow of a doubt. It filled me with wonder and a complete reverence. I had the same feeling with me as I did when I was with the nuns.

I was in my element. It all made complete sense and Miss Jones was a genius. She was also thought of a tyrant by some of the consultants. She was wiser I believe and had far more knowledge than them as she specialized in everything. Some of our class were scared of her as she spoke her mind, had very high standards and expectations, was direct and very strict.

I liked her. I got her and she got me. She took us under her wing like a mother hen. We had an interview with her every three months, after we had done a "block" of time on the ward. She interviewed both my step mum and me individually for a nursing place.

She has since come through in messages. A particular one last year in 2015 was amazing. I know that she has watched me from the Spirit world. More about that later. I don't remember any of the other tutors very well, she is the one that has remained in my memory.

I believe we all have a teacher that has inspired or helped us in some way. Who was yours?

I continued to dream at this time. I have always dreamed and I remember one dream in particular. I dreamt about an aeroplane crash. I remember seeing the aeroplane coming down and then boom. I don't recall the facts apart from the year. It was about 1981 but I remember waking up in the morning and switching on the news and there it was. I told my friend when I got to work the following morning. She said "Oh my god, do not tell Sister." I think she thought I was a bit strange anyway.

Mr Smith was a patient in his 50's that could not move anything. He was on what I recall being a special bed called a "Stryker" bed. They were not mechanical in those days but had to be worked manually. It took three of us to manoeuvre him to the toilet, to sit up to turn him over. He was a large man. Three of us were in the room; the two other nurses had been out the previous night and were nattering away about it. I felt a bit uncomfortable because poor Mr Smith was in the middle of being moved. All of a sudden, a voice said "It's your souls you need to take care of". It felt like a bolt of lightening and I got it completely and knew it. The other two nurses looked at each other and raised their eyebrows. We finished in the room. I went back in and said thank you to him. I have never forgotten his message nor the circumstances and the way in which he gave it.

A girl in our group, called Jayne, was always doing funny things caused by her nervousness. She looked like a 60's hippy chick. She spoke very nicely, had round glasses and long dark "fuzzy" hair. She burnt Joss sticks and had ethnic art and covers all over room and seemed spaced out most of the time. She was different for that time. I tried my best to help her with things, especially when she was on the same ward.

Apart from running all around the hospital looking for Nephrons (requested by goodness knows who, I am sure Karma has visited them since), one April fool's day she did one of the funniest things I have seen and which I couldn't save her from. We had old fashioned thermometers in those days with the mercury. They were kept in a cleaning solution in a small plastic box and had to be shaken down after use. It took ages and made my wrists ache. "Nurse have you shaken the thermometer's down?" It was the same Matron who happened to be on every time I was on night duty who said the same thing on every shift. Nurse!

Jayne was on the afternoon shift on the same male ward I was on as my first ward. She was asked to do the observations.   Temperature, blood pressure and respiratory observations. It was routine that all the patients had this done at this time of the day.

She got the metal trolley with her box of shaken down thermometers and proceeded to walk from the top of the ward to the bottom, putting a thermometer in all the men's mouths and then going back up to the top to take a reading. There was a problem. Instead of putting the mercury end in their mouths, she put them in the wrong way around. All of the men sat there in beds, chairs, in plasters, splints or on traction with those thermometers in the wrong way with the metal bits sticking out of their mouths, until some clever person said "Excuse me love. You have put the thermometers in the wrong way around."
The place erupted in laughter and poor Jayne disappeared.

We had been told by previous trained nurses that on results day, if you had a thin envelope in your mail box you passed. If you had a thick envelope you had failed because it contained forms for re-sitting the exam.

We all sat together in the dining room. A huge old fashioned room with high ceilings, floor to ceiling windows that let in the wind, old fashioned pipe radiators, large wooden tables, wooden floors that squeaked when you walked on them and a huge wooden door in the comer with a large round dark handle that opened beside the (scary) mail boxes, as they were that day. These were made of wood as well with pigeon holes with our name on. Waiting……

I remember Jayne that day collecting her envelope. It was a thick one. I remember sitting there hoping (even though I knew) that she had passed, but she hadn't and never did. Perhaps it was not the right job for her and I often think and wonder what she ended up doing. Perhaps something that resonated with her soul in a better way.

I believe if we are in the wrong place nothing is easy. If we are in the right place things will flow.

My training was intense, funny, inspirational, sad, horrifying, gory, stressful, depressing, fun, hard work and I grew up at nineteen. I had seen so much. I no longer believed that all old people like granddad Jim and nana and nana Terry and Granddad Don were nice and that as you grew older you became nicer. I realized this the day an elderly couple who had been together for years had to be separated in the dayroom on a medical ward because they kept throwing punches at each other.

I grew up and to some extent lost my shyness. Miss Jones, after seeing a ward report that said I was shy, said it was because I was thinking of myself. Perhaps that is true in part. I learnt to manage it. I am still shy in particularly social situations but at my age now I perhaps have now learnt to just be and to manage it.

The most beautiful part of my training and this period of my life were the people I met. After thirty or so years they are still fresh in my memory. Each of them taught me something or showed me something and perhaps showed me a part of myself that was very similar to something in them. My daughter did her training at the same hospital and now works there as a staff nurse.

I received a message from Miss Jones from the spirit world. The year was 2015 I had gone to the Arthur Findlay College for the second time with a couple of friends. I had the completely perfect teacher for me in John Johnson. He is quiet and gentle and an excellent medium.
We stood up giving messages and it was Barbara's turn. "I have got a lady here. She has got a tweed skirt on and

flat shoes. oh dear. I don't know whether I am very sure about her, she feels really harsh."
John asked "What did she do?" He was tuning in as well.
"She had something to do with medicine."
"Yes". I was squeezing my hands together and my lips because I knew exactly who it was. I don't know. Ask her. "She liked books. Somebody here knew her when they were younger." She looked at me.
"Yes, I can take her."
The Message from Ms Jones was that in some ways we were alike. As brilliant as she was as a Tutor, the other areas of her life she found difficult because she was shy. That was her message. I now know why she understood me. Again, as I write I feel her hand on my shoulder. I thank her for her understanding.

Paul – My friend who was killed on his bike.
Mr Smith - The man on the Stryker bed.
Jayne - My nursing college
Amanda – My School friend

My office colleagues:
 Susie – The office Junior
 Ingrid – The lady from Holland
 Mr Smart – The office manager
 And last but not least, Roy (the boy)

I thank them all and for some reason along the twist and turns of life they figured hugely. There are many more I haven't mentioned and more to come.
I am lucky that I have had messages from two of them from gifted mediums. Who knows, maybe there are more to come.

Chapter Seven

I got married at the tender age of 21. My first daughter was born in 1986, my son in 1988 and my youngest daughter in 1990.
I loved every minute of my children's young life but it made me acutely aware of the loss of my own mum. It was hard sometimes, but I did the best I could. I still worked as a nurse.

I spent a lot of my time working "on the bank" at weekends. I usually worked on the Oncology unit. I loved it. It was an amazing place. But also, very sad. I knew I wanted to work in a hospice and a children's hospice. Not then but later. I felt too young and wanted to mature a bit. I did both later when my family had grown up.

I found it tough looking after a family and working and I eventually, as I anticipated, became ill.

Problems began with my legs that didn't seem to go in the direction I wanted them to. I used to trip up, lose my balance and then one day could not stop being sick. I felt incredibly ill and was eventually admitted to hospital. They gave me medication to stop the sickness and I was let home. The nurse said a very strange thing when I left, she said "good luck". I went home.

A few days later, in the evening, I was in bed and felt very strange. I felt as if I was sinking and had a feeling I was going to die. I found myself out of my physical body, although I had a body. I was in a different place. Everything that I was, am, have been, my soul was encased in a bubble of energy. I was aware of others. No words were spoken, everything was transmitted by the power of thought. I did not see a light or tunnel, maybe because of my beliefs I missed this bit? And then I saw myself. I did not like what I saw. I did not like aspects of myself. I had a choice to stay or to return but I knew in that moment the choice had already been made by me. I was very aware at this time of an angelic energy with me. I came back and it was like stepping into a pair of cold wet wellies as my soul came back into my body. This was not the same as astral travelling I did as a child. My life changed from that moment on. The essence of this experience has dimmed over time but it was so profound. I felt emotional for some time afterwards and could not talk about it, as it seemed to dilute it.

I went on a mission. I read books, and I researched things. One of the first books I bought after this was Embraced by the light, by Betty Eddie. But I knew, I knew that without a shadow of a doubt we do not die. I joined the national healing federation and went on their course. During the course in a class situation, Mike who was running it, looked in my direction and asked who has had a near death experience? "I have"
"What happened"? I told him and the class. He explained that he had experienced an almost identical thing. He turned over one night to turn out the light and that was it. The essence was identical. He saw himself and did not like what he saw.

It validated the experience for me. It was also a major turning point in my life. I learnt through him and the course how psychic I was standing in a queue one day at the town hall to practise healing. I heard as clear as a bell. "You are very, very Psychic". I looked up and it was him. He had projected his thoughts and I had picked them up. Again, this was validation for me. I had stepped onto a new path and it was exactly where I was meant to be.

I have to mention Aunt Nell as well as Mike. She was a major influence in my life at this time and I believe helped me step onto the spiritual path also.

She was my husbands' mothers' aunt. She was an older school spiritualist and was a force to be reckoned with. I was very scared when I first met her, having heard so many stories about this lady who was completely honest. She spoke her mind and if she did not like you she told you so and why. I met her before my near death experience, before I had my first baby and before I met Mike.

She lived in London at 11, Trinity Rise, Tulse Hill in a huge house. The house backed onto Brockwell Park. Aunt Nell's brother worked as the head gardener there for many years. The house to all intents was a museum. Her husband Bob's family worked for Cartier's and were very wealthy, hence this huge house. Bob worked as an aircraft engineer during the war. He was always making things and was very handy. I have an old clock he made out of an old wooden aeroplane.

On the day of the visit we parked in a beautiful tree lined avenue of huge houses three stories high and more. Some of these were rented out as separate flats, as uncle Bob always used to remind us about the neighbour, a single parent family. But their house was a house.

They only occupied three rooms, the kitchen that was the original kitchen down stairs. It still had the original servant's bells that I expect were used long before Aunt Nell lived there. The top floor was unusually used as a church I believe, many years previously. Aunt Nell took me up to see it one day and it hadn't changed at all. I do not know what sort of church it was. I am sure she told me but I cannot remember.

I was 22 years old and I was petrified. The trees were overgrown the garden was neglected, and the path was made of slate like granddad Jims back garden. But it felt different. By comparison his was a postage stamp. The door was huge with black handles and stained glass windows and the trees cast scary shadows over the path. They had no phone so did not know we were coming. We had not informed them.

We stood at the front door and rang the bell. It was one of those that was sunk into the wall and needed a lot of strength in a finger or two to push it, never being quite sure if it had rung on the other side of the huge door. You could though see through the Victorian patterned glass that was ample. Uncle Bob answered. "Oh hello" he said, "We were expecting you. Nell has just put the kettle on, she is downstairs making a cup of tea. Do come in". Just like that!

I think that was my first introduction to a natural medium who thought it completely normal, as did Uncle Bob. I wasn't quite sure.

We walked in to a time machine that transported us swiftly and directly back to the Victorian days. A grandfather clock stood in the hall on the right ticking loudly next to an old brolley/coat stand that was miniature by comparison. "Coats!" said Uncle Bob.

We were shown into the parlour through a huge brown heavy looking door with a large brown handle that seemed to take forever to open. Perhaps time had stopped. Everything was dark. Dark wood, dark furniture, dark curtains, dark walls covered in old flock wallpaper. It smelt of old things and old time. There were plants on tall standing three legged tables, an old carpet covered the floor in the middle, hugged by a

wooden parquet floor. There seemed to be many things in the room lost in vastness and darkness of the space. But there was lightness in the energy amongst the heaviness of the old Victorian room. Uncle Bob perched himself up against the tall Victorian fire place. We sat down on an old leather tub sofa that was definitely antique (and dark) waiting to meet this lady who was ridiculed and spoken about harshly by her family because she was a spiritualist. I had never met one of those before.
"She will be up in a minute" (from the kitchen) said Uncle Bob after what seemed a long time of waiting. He spoke very few words and didn't believe I feel, in making conversation to be polite or for the sake of something to say. So, that was it. He didn't ask my name or anything about me. They were expecting us that was that. We waited and the clock ticked.

And in she came. She was tiny. She was built like a bird and wore a blue house coat. She had the most amazing blue eyes and a stare that looked right through you. "Hello Dear. We have been expecting you" and she smiled at me. I loved her from that moment on.
She talked about spirits, her guides, door keepers, nature spirits (yes fairies). She had them in her garden. I wasn't sure about this at the time but have since changed my mind. She had the most sensitive, fragile energy I have ever experienced and she was the most natural medium I have ever met. She glowed. She was old fashioned. A seamstress in her younger years she made couture dresses. I have her treasured wooden sewing box. She belonged to her local spiritualist Church. I don't know which one, I can't remember what she told me but there are a few in the area Stockwell, Balham and Battersea. She never worked as a medium but was a healer. She knew all the old fashioned natural remedies and she swore by them. I have her little black note book.

Below is one of them exactly as it is written in the book that is now falling apart, literally at the seams.

Slippery Elm

One ounce of bark simmered slowly in two pints of water down to one pint.
(I guess then you drink it after skimming it)
It is very beneficial in Diarrhoea, Pneumonia, Dysentery, coughs and sore throat.
It is a very valuable remedy employed in mucous inflammation of the lungs, Bowels and Stomach, Kidneys

Funnily enough, I have at this moment got a Bronchial infection and I can feel her energy as I write. Maybe I should get some. It is available today in different forms from health food shops.

She was around at the time when all the old mediums like Gordon Higginson and Harry Edwards were doing their séances and demonstrations.

I have just found a newspaper clipping of an advert to attend a healing demonstration with the famous Harry Edwards in Portsmouth in her falling apart black book.

Portsmouth

Harry Edwards Visiting
Forresters Hall,
Fratton Road.
Portsmouth.
On Saturday, July 20th, 6.30pm
Will demonstrate
Spiritual Healing
Admission by ticket 1/- W.E Moule

We became friends over the years and she helped me immensely. She was though, a force to be reckoned with because she just knew and spoke her mind. I saw her tell somebody off and it was sharp, to the point and she wasn't changing her mind. She was right. She always wore a hat with a pin in it and her bony fingers had a knack of getting it in the right place first time.

Aunt Nell took me to my first spiritualist church near Brighton, where my parents in law lived at the time. I was very excited and also a bit nervous as I had never been inside a spiritualist church before. We sat near the back, that was my choice. I did not want any attention and I did not want a message. She had already told me I would get one. I did but before then (I was the last message), she started doing her Aunt Nell thing "I do not like him. That is not good medium ship, its rubbish", tutting and blowing her nose on a hankie. We were at the back and her intention was that she could be heard along with her disapproval.

I then heard the medium say "Hello". I sank down in my chair. I knew from the way he said it was my Grandma Terry with a message about a house move (which came true). So, that was my first experience of a Spiritualist Church. I never thought that I would one day be standing at the front doing the same thing and luckily, I have not had any Aunt Nells in the audience. Only beside me from the spirit world, usually in the car with me on my journeys.

After this first meeting I used to receive parcels in the post from Aunt Nell. I had struggled with the girls' hair for some time and could not find a hair brush that did not hurt. A knock came on the door one day. It was the post man with a parcel amongst other things, and inside was the most beautiful hair brush made of ivory and natural bristle. I have it today and wondered where it was as I was writing this. I opened a drawer this morning and there it was.

She stayed with us in our home after Uncle Bob had died, for Christmas. She was 89 years old. We lived on the edge of a small town very near the country. She loved trees. We had row of them framing our long driveway. She liked the energy of them. Wrapping ourselves against the cold, we went for a walk. It was a crisp cold day, one of those days when the cobwebs freeze and the grass sparkles with the frost, when the earth seems to have been sprinkled with a magic wand turning it into a sparkly wonderland.

She wanted to go in the fields. "We have to climb over stiles Aunt Nell" I said, wondering if her little elderly frame could manage it. Absolutely! Was she going! She was not deterred and off we went climbing over stiles across fields. For a lot of the time she had her arm through mine. "Why is my arm buzzing?"
"It's healing" she said. This was my first introduction to healing. She stopped and spoke to all the creatures and insects along the way, "Hello little spider. God bless you."

"Why is it when I am with you, things happen?" I asked her one morning after waking up to one of those experiences you never forget. She somehow heightened my sensitivity. I woke up one night when she was living at my parents in law and we were visiting. By my bedside I could see lots of little sparkles that radiated the most beautiful energy. I asked her what it was. "Oh, it was an angel" she said, matter-of-factly.

I had dreams. We were in a tunnel, Aunt Nell and myself, and had just witnessed a car crash. We were both out of our bodies. A young man had died and his

soul had already moved on. "There is nothing we can do for him" she said. I am not sure for definite what we were supposed to do, but I sensed guide him gently on his way, as he would have left his body quite quickly.
She spoke about her guide often and because of my curiosity I really wanted to see him. I looked and looked and thought I saw in my minds eye a Chinese man with a short plait. All of a sudden, she turned around and said "And don't you go looking for his plait he has had it cut", amazing such was her sensitivity. She knew what I was doing and what I thought I had seen and I was wrong and she told me.

She had an old chest of drawers that belonged to her mother. I believe it was a wedding present. It was made of dark mahogany wood with bun feet and round handles with dovetail hinges. It stood tall and looked very proud and solid. It was also at this time at least over a hundred years old (Aunt Nell was 89) and I loved it. As I mentioned before, I loved old furniture, particularly Victorian.

I sat talking to her one day in her bedroom where this piece of furniture sat. She looked at me all of a sudden and said "That will be yours one day." It is, along with her favourite pieces of furniture and books.

I went into my father in laws garden shed a couple of years later. The chest of drawers sat there in its home of cold and damp. It held all tools, screws, hammers, paint brushes and other things. It was being used as a huge tool box. All I kept thinking is, it's going to get ruined I in here, so I asked him if I could have it. To my surprise, he said yes.

It is now in a bedroom in my home (as predicted), being loved and used as it was intended to be. When we moved, I was offered some money for it by the removal man who fell in love with it as well, but I wouldn't part with it.

She was taken into hospital at 89 years and did not go home. I knew when she was unconscious and near to death. I saw her wander into my kitchen and disappear. Having always believed throughout my nursing career that the spirit can leave the body when a person is unconscious (and at other times), this experience verified my belief.

I am lucky. I know she is near, although in recent years I have not felt her presence quite so much, apart from when I was writing about her black book and her recipe Slippery Elm. I believe she has moved onto higher realms. She looked forward to going home and being reunited with Bob. She will be very busy in the spirit world.

She had a profound belief in God and she was closer to the spirit world than anyone else I had met up until that time.
I opened her Black book one day and a poem fell out. It is called "Because of you x".

Chapter Eight

Finding a Spiritualist Church happened naturally after meeting Mike and enrolling on a Healing course. I was invited to a church by a man and lady there, who became friends. The Church was in the town of Shrewsbury next to Rackham's, just off the high street. I was nervous. It was like walking into Aunt Nells house all over again. It felt ancient, the man who ran it looked ancient and the lady medium looked ancient. It was very old fashioned. There was a pulpit, a hymn board and books and it again smelt of oldness. I really don't know or remember exactly what happened, but I enjoyed the service and it but more important, it led me on to the next stage in my development.

I was invited to a circle by Janet, at her home, the following Monday. We all sat around seeing what we could pick up. When it was my turn, I saw a church steeple. That was it, nothing more or less. I was again, that evening, given validation and confirmation that the Spirit world existed in a message from my 7 year old niece, who had died tragically by being hit by a van. The message was from Janet.

I do not want to go into details, but one thing in that message was so accurate, I knew without a shadow of a doubt.

Today I feel the same. It is all in the evidence; just a few small details can change a person's life. My life changed again that evening.
I continued to sit in circle and to develop. The information I got was correct and I seemed to have a gift for remote viewing. I use this today and can go into

peoples' houses, drawers and books with their permission, of course.

Marg was an elderly local medium, a bit of a character and very well known in the area. Janet asked her along to circle one evening. They were friends. Marg ran a circle and Janet was once one of her fledglings. She was a cockney lady and reminded me in some ways of Aunt Nell. Very to the point and direct, she quite often got into trouble in the spiritualist churches for her directness. She gave what she got and didn't change it or mess with it. She went to a lady once with a message from her husband "He lived in muck and died in muck". He was a farmer and this is exactly how he spoke. Why change it? It was simple and perfect evidence. I will talk about this later.

Marg came to Janet's circle and asked a question "Whoever can tell me this is a very good medium. Who can tell me what my husband did?" I didn't need to think about it, and image popped into my mind of a man knitting. "He used to knit." Being sensitive, I could also feel the displeasure of one or two of the group.

Janet rang me the next day. "Marg would like to see you. Fancy going this week?" We turned up at a prefabricated bungalow. It had net curtains up at the window that were yellow. Marg smoked very heavily. The curtains were yellow and so were the walls and everything else. It was a tiny simple place with a living room, kitchen and a bedroom. She lived on her own as her husband had died.
"Hello love"
"Hello Marg". We chatted for a while and she gave me a reading. She brought my mum through and I could feel her energy. She mentioned a name that I called my husband (it was quite rude). I was amazed. Nobody in

their wildest imaginations could have guessed, let alone have known what it was. She also told me "You are going to be a very famous medium one day and become very well known. You are very, very good but you need to find a Spiritualist Church." I did this some years later but at the time I didn't believe a word of it.

I lost touch with Marg for a while, but heard through the grapevine three years later that she was poorly. I decided to ring her. "Hello Marg. I don't know if you remember me? It's Caroline."
"Hello love"
"I am just ringing to see how you are?" We talked and all of a sudden, she said "My husband said he will let me know he is ok and that the spirit world exists by giving his name." I didn't say anything but put the phone down.

Then it started. I had her husband with me. He was singing in my ear "I am Bernard. Bernard is my name". He would not go away for some time. It reminded me of the scene in ghost when Sam was trying to talk to Whoopie Goldberg. I never rang her to tell her that Bernard was with me, and always regretted it, but I am sure that Bernard used another medium to get his message across. He was very determined and I am also sure they are together in the spirit world and she knows it exists.

Chapter Nine

I was introduced to the Arthur Finlay College of Psychic Science at Stanstead by Janet, who went along with another circle member. I had never heard of it. It was not time for me to go (I did later). It was the first time I heard of names like Mavis Patilla, Paul Jacobs, Lynn Coterrall, Eileen Davis and others. I was to meet and attend classes quite a few years later with some of these people. It opened doors for me and on my second visit I was invited to work in Norway.

After being ill, I was unable to go back into nursing and needed to focus on something else. Nana Terry had also died and this sent me into some sort of an anxious state. I couldn't sit still or settle to do anything. I went to the doctors who said it was reactive and would pass. He gave me some "happy pills". I did not take them, but instead enrolled in the study of something that had always fascinated me because of granddad Jims stories about the Italian prisoners that he was in charge of at Harporley POW and because of the man he was. People and Psychology. It worked. My anxiety stopped.

I decided and it stipulated in the advertisement for the course that you first had to enrol and pass the introductory course. So I did. I never liked talking about myself, was hopeless at talking up in a group and had a pathological fear of standing up in front of people. I was comfortable and happy, as I still am today, just listening.

We sat in a circle. "I would like you all just to introduce yourselves and tell me why you are here". I have said this so many times myself since and look out for the uncomfortable people. I sat three quarters around this circle and it started. I could feel my blood pressure go up. My heart started beating in my chest so loudly I was sure everyone could hear, my hands were shaking and I was the colour of beetroot. I would have done anything to make the floor swallow me up at that moment. It got worse as my turn came around. I was always the same in groups in that situation. Our tutor was taking notes.

The course lasted for 12 weeks and we had assignments to do. I failed the first one and got a D. I was not used to the university format or clear about what was required. But it inspired me and I loved it. It was everything I had imagined and more. I was learning about people and myself.

Sarah was Irish and about the same age as me. She was a teacher in a catholic school for girls that was run by nuns (Catholic theme again). She was an excellent teacher. Her knowledge was amazing and just like Miss Jones' Anatomy and Physiology class (although she was very different; she was married with children where as Miss Jones was a definite Ms.), I was absolutely enthralled.

I decided I wanted to do the next stage up, a two year course. I was interviewed by Sarah and got accepted. I loved it. I was definitely in the right place, it felt so right. I loved research and reading and critically analysing theories and concepts. I found the anatomy and physiology lessons I had when I was doing my nurse training helped to understand the biological reasons for abnormal behaviour but most of all for me, I was learning about the fundamentals of humans. Why do they behave in the way they do? How can I react to the behaviour? What words can I use to help them and understand them and also myself? That was the reason for doing it. It gave me everything and more and helped me understand.

Quite often in the following years, when I was going through a difficult time with understanding a person and their behaviour and how to deal with it on a personal level, I would hear 'remember what you have learnt'.

I became friendly with Mary who was also doing the course, and to my astonishment she had been a nun! Her brother was a priest who lived in Brazil looking after the homeless children and the poor, who touched hands with the better off. My children and I used to send them toys and things for the children. We used to raid cupboards, have sort outs and go to the sweet shop and buy sweets and put them in envelopes. We received letters and photos back. The children were beautiful but had no one special to love them.

Mary was lovely. I met her in Birmingham before our graduation. What a grand affair that was. I loved it! There was an orchestra with wonderful speeches. One of the proudest moments was when our group was introduced. We were more mature than the majority of students and it was said the hardest time to study is when you are older, with more demands from families and work. This group should be so proud of their achievements. I was, we were. I passed with an 'A' for my final project, a dissertation on M.A. I wanted to pack it in so many times. It was tough but my steely determination won through, as did the help and encouragement of Sarah. After our graduation, Mary and I lost touch.

Sometimes I believe that people are only meant to be in our lives for a moment and then you go on your pathway and them on theirs. It can be quite difficult letting go sometimes, but when we look at it in this way it is easier and meant to be.

It doesn't mean we forget them, it just means it is time to move on and allow different people to come in. I also believe very strongly that the longer we hold onto a situation-it could be a job, a relationship and social group, and we know deep down or have that gut feeling it is not right for us, perhaps people are being difficult, we feel uncomfortable or we have a niggle about something but can't quite put it into words, these are all signs to have a look at the situation and perhaps think it is time to move on. I have seen and experienced this myself. I have ignored it and then ignored it again and then something will happen and I have no choice but to leave. It can be that someone has been underhanded and caused you great upset or as a last resort you will become ill. Looking back, it is amazing to see what a blessing that was, that a person underhanded you or you were ill because it moved you onto a new stage of your journey, even though it was very painful at the time. I explain a little bit more about this later on.

I have met so many people in my life who, like Mary and Sarah, have stepped onto my path at a major turning point in my life to help me onto the next stage. When I look back and as I am writing this, I realize I had almost forgotten them. They have been in the periphery of my memory as I draw the memory of them close to my thoughts and into my heart. I feel a sense of being blessed and also wonder at the synchronicity that they were there at that time.

Can you remember anyone in your past that was there at a particular moment or a difficult period when circumstances moved you on?

Has anyone been behind you and gently encouraged you in something that you have found difficult?

Chapter Ten

There was no end to my thirst for knowledge after my near death experience. After completing the Psychology course, I decided to enrol on another course. An Introduction to counselling.

Again, I loved it. I met two people on that course; Chris and Debs. We had many good times the three of us. Chris was older with grown up nearly children. Robin, her husband, was an illustrator. They lived in London but had moved to the Shropshire countryside where they had bought an old house. Chris created a beautiful garden and Robin had a studio in an old barn that he did his work from.

Debs. I love Debs. she is mother earth personified, a beautiful soul. she is a free spirit and at the time was bringing up five Children on her own. To my wishy washy floaty ways, she was and is the complete opposite. Practical, grounded and down to earth. She trained as a reflexologist and is an amazing healer.

We lost touch for 10 years. I walked into a shop 6 months ago, on a visit to Shropshire that did not have a pair of jeans in my size in my shop locally, and said to the assistant "Could you tell me if you have any jeans in this size?"
"Caroline!!!"
"Debs!!!" It was one of those amazing magic moments that was definitely engineered, and also her last day in the shop. I wondered about her for years. how she was, how she was doing? And tried to find her but I never had any luck and then I bumped into her. We are now in touch, although living in different parts of the country

and I believe that we have a few more things to do. Watch this space.

Have you ever bumped into someone completely unexpected out of the blue in amazing circumstances?

I have already mentioned Mike and the weekend courses with the NFH (National Federation of Healers). This course was different. It ran for two years. The lady who ran it was a psychotherapist and a healer and also a nutritionist. Chris rang me up one day and told me about a course she was going to do. She mentioned the word Karma and that was it, I knew I had to do it. I knew it was the course for me. There was though, a slight problem. It had already started.
"Ring Ann up" said Chris, so I did.
"No I am sorry" she said "it has already started." I rang Chris. "She said no, it has already started"
"Ring her again!" I did and I explained that I really wanted to do it, it felt right for me. "Come and see me" she said.

I drove to see her. Later on, she said to me "I have never met anyone so determined and yet it was very strange. You turned up and were so quiet." I didn't have the heart to tell her I had been badgered by Chris. I am glad she did. I got on the course. It again was a major learning curve for me.

I realized I was aware of energy naturally. We learnt so much. Karma, meditation of different sorts and the physiological affects on the body, chakras, Psychology again, counselling skills. We did exercises with energy, sending it, receiving it (healing is energy), brain waves, sleep patterns, so many interesting things but the most important thing the healing course was based on, is "Healer heal thyself". So many people go into the

Spiritual realms, healing with unresolved emotional stuff. It's always, in my opinion, far better to start work with a clean slate.

Ann's counselling course was on at the same time as the healing course but was a weekend course. It was slightly different in that it covered everything a conventional counselling course covered, but it also covered things like astrology, in particular planetary aspects at birth. This is very different from looking at daily horoscopes and was surprisingly, to my querying mind, very accurate.

It gave us an indication as to what our major learning is in this lifetime. Mine was, and I was amazed at this, the loss of a mother. I still have my chart today and it is very interesting. I did not know my time of birth (which is necessary to do an accurate chart), so Ann used her pendulum. I found out later that the pendulum was correct or the force behind it was correct. That was interesting. So, the astrologers of ancient times were perhaps far more advanced in a lot of ways than we are.
I realized something major on this course, that actually, we have all experienced the same hurts, just in a different setting or a different stage.

How many of you have experienced a broken relationship, jealousy, anger, the loss of a pet or a loved one? Perhaps you have more in common with your neighbour than you think.

So, Chris, myself and Debs did this course. We really had some fun and again learnt so much. As part of the course, we had to have Psychotherapy (a bit difficult helping someone if you have had the same problem and not resolved, it a bit like a recipe for disaster). We could choose who we wanted to see. I had no idea. I did not know any Psychotherapists apart from the one who was sitting in front of me. I wanted to ask her but didn't, well not yet anyway. So, I asked Ann if she could recommend someone and she did.

I went for two sessions with this lady and on the third session, I turned up at this lovely lady's house but immediately knew she had had a row with her husband. Ooo dear, I felt extremely uncomfortable. She was not in the right frame of mind to be seeing me, I could feel it. Having had some experience of counselling and energy, I knew the idea was to create an empty space. It wasn't empty and didn't feel right. I didn't go back.

I asked Ann if she would take me on she said yes. What an experience. There is a reason for everything. We went through my childhood and she didn't see any major issues (compared to some childhoods she said), so she asked me if we could do a past life regression under hypnosis. I still have a copy of this and it is fascinating. She was interested that I was a twin from a spiritual perspective, that I had come into this life with another soul at the same time and we had also shared a womb.

She started on a journey in the womb through all the trimesters. Being a twin but not identical, this space was shared with my sister who, even before birth was bigger, and stronger than me and probably more dominant. I went to twelve weeks when I knew I could have died due to lack of nourishment (this has been confirmed). My mum nearly lost one of us or both at this time.

She then took me back to before I was born and to the relationship I had with my sister in a previous life. I will not divulge the details here but it made complete and utter sense and I knew it was real. I have understood her since then, perhaps in a way I never did before. I have complete understanding of our relationship and the reason for us being together in this life time. I also knew when we went back to pre-birth I did not want to come here. I knew that I would find my life hard. Interestingly, when you look at pictures of both my sister and me, she is grinning from ear to ear, full of beans. When look at me and I am smiling quietly as if to say I am not quite sure about this.

The last question Ann asked me at the end of my session was "What is your reason for being here?" My answer "knowing", "what are you" and "light".

She brought me back and looked at me. "It is an honour and privilege to meet you."

I did not need to go back to see Ann.

If we can think of our soul as having many journeys, adventures and learning many lessons in different bodies, then it means the soul does not die. Each life time is not a single lifetime but a continuous experience through birth and death of different bodies. After each incarnation, we travel home for a little while and then take a new journey to a new destination in a new vehicle, our bodies, until it wears out or for some reason stops working. Our souls or ourselves leave and go home again.

The soul will bring its own experience of a past life with a different body and whilst in a body the soul and body merge as one. Therefore, it makes sense that a body will be affected by the soul energy that inhabits it. Because everything is energy, thoughts and feelings are less dense but will eventually be expressed through the physical body.

I read a book after this called "Many lives many Masters" it was written by the American Psychologist Brian Weiss, who I think was probably one of the first eminent medical professionals to come out about there being something else to look at than just the personality/brain when treating people with emotional problems. This happened quite by accident with one of his patients called Catherine. She brought past life information forward and also messages from the masters.

He regressed his patients. He believed after hearing some of the information that came from his patients that a lot of emotional problems we have are due to unresolved trauma in previous lives. This, since that time, has become very popular amongst some of the general population. I am not sure about the medical profession. Although I do know from experience that a lot of doctors are very intuitive, they are not able to express it.

A fellow intuitive person will recognise and sense another intuitive person. I have seen this in the medical profession and I would like to add I believe these people make the best doctors when knowledge and gut feeling are used in conjunction and sit together as one in diagnosing and treatment.

I have also experienced the opposite when someone has sat in front of me and used a "tick sheet". This, believe me, works not half as well. Me with my intuition sitting there and saying "How about antibiotics?" because my whole body is screaming infection, infection and I know it would be to my advantage to have them. Was my intuition correct? Yes. I developed a chest infection.

I think on the whole we use our intuitions far more than we realize. I also think that the medical profession is so scared of getting it wrong because of the climate we live in and follow the guidelines to the tee, perhaps because of fear.

Fear. This I believe, is one of the biggest negative emotions that creates so many problems and obstacles. It roots us literally to the spot in any given moment, situation, experience or time. It is the complete opposite of faith. When you continuously live in fear you have no faith. Faith is the belief that something else exists that is far bigger and greater than us. Something that we can call on in times of need, to sort things out and believing that this thing that is far greater than us is all knowing and seeing.

Moving on from this faith is believing that in every experience there is something to be learnt or gained. Someone living in fear will think that every "bad" situation is the end of there world. Someone living in faith will see this as a challenge or a learning experience. What can I gain or learn from this?

Faith breeds positivity. Fear breeds negativity. Faith flows. Fear is rigid. Faith takes chances because it just feels right and everything will be ok. Fear does not take chances because it is too risky and everything will fall apart.

Both of these, fear and faith, will get you where you are meant to be on your pathway (nothing can stop you going where you are meant to be). But one of these will get you there probably without too much angst and the other may not be quite so easy because of the fear and the emotions that involves. But it is always good to remember that a bit of both in balance is a good thing.

Chapter Eleven

It is a known fact that in times of great difficulty we will say "Oh God help me". I have done it myself. One of my biggest requests in these moments is "Please, give me a sign". I need a sign so that I know which path to take, what to do, say and every other answer I would like to help to solve a problem or have it solved for me. So, I look for the sign. Can I see it? Nope. So, I ask again "Please give me another sign, I didn't see the last one". I wait. Nothing.

But it is there. The spirit world never ever let you down, ever. It is there when you turn on the television and hear someone talk. It is on the bus/tube/train/aeroplane when you over hear someone mention a name. It is on the radio in a song, open a book randomly and it is there. How do you know it is a sign? Because you feel it right in the centre of your solar plexus. You just know. Do you act on it? First you have got to recognise it. That requires faith or a belief in something bigger. Otherwise, you will probably not recognise it and keep asking "Where are you I need your help!" It is there all of the time in every moment this is faith.

As you believe, so you will see the magic in every day. Synchronicities will become more apparent, the unseen magic that weaves its way into the corners of our existence and touches our lives in unbelievable ways, prying and popping out gently, unexpectedly in every experience, touching our hearts and souls with joy. This can be seen as the flat, uninspiring, meek, tepid experience of 'it's a coincidence' or the wondrous, magical, miracle of the spirit world showing us they are there.

Have you experienced a synchronicity or coincidence so unexpected in its relevance that it amazed you?

Five years later

I was now living down South with my second husband to be, Peter. This had been predicted by a very good friend and medium a year before but I was having none of it. Here I was. A new place. A new area and a new start.

This occurred and was engineered, I believe, by circumstances beyond our control. I had found a job and felt the need to find a church as was told by Aunt Nell and Marg in previous years. This now happened.

I rang various churches up but they didn't feel quite right. I then rang a church up in the city of Bath and left a message. Lucy rang back. I knew this was the right one when she said "We are here to help people and move them forward" she said. And that is exactly what they did.

The circle started on the following Tuesday and she asked if I would like to go along so that I could meet them and they could meet me. I went but I could not find the church. It was behind Marks and Spencer's down a side street. It was a particularly rainy evening and I was soaked. Eventually I found it, an obscure green door amongst lots of other doors with no sign. I was half an hour late and they had started. Doors locked promptly at 7.00pm.

I went the following week and I loved it. No messing. Again, if people were not right they were there one week and gone the next. I am not sure what the criteria was but I seemed to fit the bill.

I always find this a very interesting subject. There are so many circles, development groups and courses that are very expensive (these are usually healing courses). I listen to what they entail; learning and working with chakras, symbols, signs and many other things but you know, I really do believe that whatever we attach to it, it all uses exactly the same energy.

I also think we forget that we, as humans, do not own it. We are merely the channels through which it works. We have no control over how it works, where it goes or if it works. There is nothing special about it, after all it is the most natural thing in the world. It is a pure energy similar to the energy of love.

Some of the most amazing healers, for example Harry Edwards, did not learn about healing. He was connected to the spirit world and working closely with them he was able to perform the most amazing miracles. I am sure he did not take any credit for his work. He was purely the channel through which the spirit world worked.

I heard a story once about a baker. He was a very humble man and a natural healer. People used to go and see him for ailments that they had. He was well known where he lived for his ability to cure. He had many people who wanted to see him and was very much in demand. He did not attend any courses but I suspect he was consciously or unconsciously connected to the spirit world.

I used to know a lady called Margaret. She was like the baker, very down to earth, humble and lived a very simple life. She owned very little. She rented a couple of rooms next to a railway line. It was comfortable and basic. She was also a smoker like Marg and used to puff on a cigarette in between taking a breath and talking. My friends and I used to go and see her. She used to spread her ancient tarot cards out on her little round table and give a reading. She said it exactly as it was.

I was learning to develop myself at that time and remember asking her once "How do you work Margaret?" She just looked at me "Oh I don't know love. I just do it. I don't know how I do it". There is a lot to be said for that and a lot to be said for just letting it flow and being with it. It is natural and man quite often interferes with it by putting labels on it or it should be done this way or that. She didn't think about or analyze how she was doing it. She just did it and she was an amazing psychic.

I do believe though, that certain techniques can help and I am sure that as long as the healers and mediums intentions are pure then whatever "system" is used it will work just fine. It is all about love and intention. Not money, fame or ego.

I did my Sd1 and then I started my PAS platform accreditation Scheme (These are courses run by the National Spiritualist Union). For me it was ideal as it helped me get over my fear of speaking in public. This is where it really all began for me.

With encouragement and guidance at long last I started platform work. And my journey to being a public medium. It was slow and nerve wracking as I was naturally shy. Never in my wildest nightmares would I ever have imagined standing up in front of people. But with that steely determination I did it.

We had to do 25 church services and talks and had a little book to be signed. This was the beginning eight years ago. I still serve some of those first churches and met some wonderful people who gave us the opportunity and welcomed us so warmly with nothing but encouragement and love. Also, to Lucy and her husband who did exactly what they said they would with encouragement and loving guidance. I will be forever grateful.

I have been in so many Churches, all of them are different but their services all run along the same guidelines. There are five things that a medium is asked to do; an opening prayer, a reading, Philosophy, Medium ship and a closing prayer.

I found the mediumship fairly easy and the reading but the rest we were asked to stand and just talk arggghhh! I teamed up with Daisy. She is very different from me; outgoing, a chatterbox, bubbly with the most beautiful energy and she loves to talk. We did our services together for five years. Yep you got it, I ducked out of the philosophy every time and she loved it. I did the medium ship which she didn't love so much. It worked beautifully but was not ideal as eventually we were assessed individually on both.

I met Daisy at the circle in the church in Bath. She joined a few months after me and came from upstairs. This was where the beginners circle was run on the same evening. I recall, and so does she, when I said "We are going to be working together one day". I really don't know what she thought about that but we did work together for the first five years of our platform work.

We had some fun, we got lost, were late leaving by my reckoning (I needed at least to get there an hour before) and Daisy without fail always got a text "where are you?" We had problems with Sat navs, one way streets, traffic lights and every other thing that was on the roads. How we ever got any where I will never know. Daisy quite often drove, although we tried to take it in turns. I need to concentrate when I'm driving and Daisy didn't mind talking all the way so again it worked well.

I quite often used to say very calmly "Daisy you have just missed the turning?" and every time, without fail, where ever we where she would slam on her brakes and go into meltdown. We stopped dead in the middle of green lights, one way systems and motorway junctions. My reaction? "Its ok we just need to turn around. Don't worry about the traffic behind, to the side in front, it will all be fine". We also, on long journeys, spent some time looking for toilets (she explained she suffered from a weak bladder). "There's one there!"
"Where?" Slam! But we always got there safely somehow.

We were invited to do a service in Cirencester at 11.00am one Sunday morning and missed the exit on the motorway. At that exact moment, Peter rang. He gave us instructions of how and where to go by using Google maps. Parking was a problem though. Cirencester, as beautiful as it is, has a one-way system. We had five minutes to spare and just left the car in a huge car park. We did not know where we were or where the church was. I asked the first man we saw if he knew where the local Spiritualist was. "What is that?"
"It's a church. We talk to dead people". I couldn't think of any better way in such a rush to explain it. He walked off. We did get there. Daisy did the Philosophy. Her talk was very funny. It was about our journey and how we all need a Peter.

Lovely evening, it went well and we both loved it but a one hour journey took us four hours to get home. Daisy was driving. The reason it took so long was there was a main road shut for roadworks. A diversion took us in a huge circle down country lanes, hills, small road and loads of junctions until we got back to the same road works. The same flashing worker's lorry who had sent us off to get back to them a couple of hours later. I laughed so much (I was not driving) and did not need to go to the toilet. Daisy was not so amused. She'd had a busy day and wanted to get home. We got home eventually and that is how it was.

It was really sad when we went our own ways. But after five years of spending more time together than sometimes with our husbands, we decided it was time to do our own thing. I missed Daisy's company on long drives. It can be lonely but it was necessary for us both to go our separate ways. We supported each other for a long time. She was my critic and I was hers when we felt a bit flat, if we felt a service or an aspect of it didn't go very well we gave each other encouragement. We still do things together and it is always a joy and pleasure when this happens.

She said goodbye during a visit to the AFC College and was in pieces. "Caroline, I just want to say thank you for all your help and support. I would never have been able to do what I can without having your help. You have been so good to me". I think what she doesn't realize is, that I would not have been able to do it without her either. She did the philosophy for me (I only took it on when I felt confident enough) and I did the same with the Clairvoyance for her. It helped us both in the best way possible. As I write this, my phone has just gone off. It is Daisy confirming a service this Sunday.
Have you had a friend who has helped you in some way and you them without realizing how perfectly it worked until you think about it later?

My first service

I really don't know why I bothered at the time. That steely determination cropped up again. It did not take up two hours on a Sunday, it took up a whole week of chewing on it, getting completely worked up and thoughts of it seeping into every day life at any moment. I think nerve racking was not a good description, it was overwhelming.

The first service was at my local church on a Sunday evening. Lucy and her husband were with us. One of them was chairing but I don't recall which and we were asked to turn up at 6.00pm (prompt).

Have you ever felt so nervous that even picking clothes turns into a crisis? Time doesn't just move, it gallops when really, all you want it to do is stop. That is what happened. I arrived at the church and we sat in a little room deciding who was going to do what. I picked Clairvoyance. There were four of us. It happened and it went surprisingly well. I recall giving two messages and the information was taken but it took me a long time to stop getting so chewed up about it.

We started out in churches where nobody really knew us. Sometimes there were 6 people, sometimes there were 20 (that seemed a huge number). It didn't really matter to me as I always felt who ever was there was meant to be there.

There was one lady in the audience later on when I was working on my own who wanted a certain person to come through. Unfortunately, I brought her husband through.
"Well you can tell him to go away. I don't want to talk to him" She was obviously very angry at something he had done. I felt he had come to apologize but she was not

having any of it. I had to send him away. However, amazingly a few months later I met her again at a fayre I was doing. She came up with some of her family members and asked me if I could give her a reading. Her husband came through again but this time she was ready to hear from him. He was able to apologise. It was one of the most healing readings I have done. The time was right.

Had she not been there at the demonstration that evening, she would not have got a message, even an unwanted one, and she would not have then turned up at my table. So even what sometimes turns out to be negative to start with usually ends up really well. The spirit world are very clever. I believe he was meant to come through that evening to spur on another sitting where proper communication could take place and with it emotional healing.

I once went to a fayre and an elderly lady sat down at my table. "Your husband is here" I said to her. I then went on to describe him. Her daughter who she had lost, joined him and then her mother. After I had finished the reading she sat with her arms folded. "Anybody else?" "Well your husband has been, your dad has been and your daughter". She walked off. Later on, I learnt that she had asked for her money back. We cannot just drum up people. We are not in the driving seat and I am sure that whatever message and any healing that may have been given that day was completely lost in her desire to hear from one particular person.
I did for a while, feel as if I had failed and my confidence was knocked. It took me some time to get it back again. These things happen though, to either move us on or to help us look at things differently.

I seem to have a lot of communications with children. I think perhaps it is because I lost my niece when she was seven in tragic circumstances. I also love children and nothing could ever be worse that losing a child. This is a particular message that stood out. I had no idea of what it was all about to start with, I just knew it was cantered around a hospice as I saw this. As it went on it was like a story, an event in a part of the gentleman's life unfolded.

I did not know before I started to give the message that he worked in the hospice. The little boy told me and showed me a cup with a lid and a bendy straw and then I saw a picture of this gentleman going around with a tea trolley as a volunteer. This is what happened.
I stood at the front of the church and could feel a little boy with me. He had a bandage around his head. I sent out a thought and asked what is the bandage was for. The answer came back the little boy had a brain tumour. "Has anybody here had anything to do with a hospice?" A man put his hand up. "I have a little boy here who has a bandage around his head. He had a brain tumour. Do you understand this?"
"Yes"
"He is saying he had to have a lid on his tea with a bendy straw in it. You worked in the hospice as a volunteer and used to give out the teas".
"Yes" he said.
"The little boy was called Ben. He is telling me about his teddy bear. He used to have a sticker on it and bandages on his right arm the same as Ben because every time the nurses did something to Ben they did it to his teddy bear".
"Yes" he said. "
He says that his teddy bear was put in his coffin. He wants to say thank you to you for being so kind to him".

I cannot put into words or relay the full impact of this message because not only do I give information out, I feel the emotion from, in this case, Ben. The love, his energy and compassion towards this man. But I know when the communication is completely pure and not tainted by the mediums mind, usually through a lack of confidence and doubt as to what they are receiving. The whole room can feel the energy. It is in these moments incredible. It feels like everyone is one and you can hear a pin drop. The message I was getting and which was important for this man was that although he went around with the teas, he was far kinder to this little boy Ben and gave him so much in the little time he was with him than others did who had the time. Amazing. He then told me other things. He talked about his brother and his daddy. I love it when children come through, especially as it has such an impact on everyone and can be truly healing.

Chapter Twelve

Home readings began to become more frequent. I found it was word of mouth or someone had seen me demonstrate at either a church or a hall.

One of the most memorable readings I did was for a lady who had lost her sister. I gave her a short message in a clairvoyance demonstration and she rang up and asked for a reading. I cannot go into great detail for privacy reasons but this lady said it changed her life for the better. Because of some of the detail she was able to believe that her sister was with her.

I feel as if I need to mention honesty. It is such an important tool that we all have. It creates a feeling of solidness within your own being because it aligns with your soul. It takes courage to be honest and also vulnerability. But it creates healthier relationships.
Dishonesty creates confusion in every sphere of life. Where there is dishonesty there is confusion. Which is why I insist on honesty when I am working with the spirit world.

Dishonesty and being economical with the truth creates assumptions and these are never the truth. But perhaps when people make assumptions it tells us more about others and where they are on their spiritual pathway. The only person who can tell the truth is the person in question, so perhaps it is better to be honest in the first place.

When I do a demonstration of any kind I ask for two things, a yes or a no. Nothing could be less complicated. I work with the spirit world, I am the middle man between you and them. We both work very hard to make it happen and the fact that it does is a miracle in itself. I have often gone to someone and they have said yes to some information and it isn't correct. How do I know that? Because my energy dips, my link with spirit loosens and the communication weakens. I know it does not feel right in my solar plexus. So, in a situation like this, I will say it does not feel right. These five words in themselves has an affect of bringing my energy back into sync with that of the spirit world. By being honest.

I was giving a demonstration in a church and I kept seeing fruit pastels. I was aware I had a lady with me and the lady was called Margaret. I said "Who knows a lady in the spirit world that liked fruit pastels? Her name was Margaret". A lady put her hand up. "I do but she liked chocolate buttons".
"I am really sorry. I can't change fruit pastels into chocolate buttons" (because that is what I was seeing). I had to be honest and I had to be sure and confident of what I was seeing. The message was taken by the correct person. If I had doubted myself and thought 'mmm perhaps what I am seeing is wrong', I would have got into a pickle. That is not to say I have not got in a pickle previously.

The spirit world are very clever. Quite often, you can start off a communication with a name and description. "I have Fred here. He was going bald, he smoked very heavily and passed with breathing problems because of his smoking". How many people in a room of sixty could take that information? Perhaps three? Three hands go up. "He lived in a terraced house". The three hands stay up. "He had a park next to his house". They stay up. "He wore glasses because he was very short sighted". They stay up and now it begins to get quite humorous (and astonishing). "He got medals for his effort in the war and he had a picket fence around his front garden that he used to paint every year". They stay up. "His wife was called Lilly and he grew lilies in the garden". Two hands go down. I now have the correct person who the message was meant for. Or do I?

Some of the above could be classed as being generic. How many of us know Fred's, who smoked and had breathing problems? Quite a few of you I expect. But if you are in a room of sixty people and everyone wants a message, how amazing is it that three people can take half of the information. I do believe the spirit world will work in the most amazing way to get a message to as many people as possible and in a situation like the above, that does not happen very often, where not everyone will get an individual message. I personally find this communication amazing. It shows the intelligence of the spirit world.

Everything that we need in a communication is given in the first image, feeling or thing we hear (Clairaudience, Clairsentience or Clairvoyance).

In a demonstration, I was shown a train. It was a Hornby train. It was kept in an attic room and was laid out permanently on the floor (I could see these images clairvoyantly). The man was an uncle. I sensed him beside me (clairsentience), who had a passion for trains. The young man at the back of the room put his hand up. I stayed in my mind in the room where the train was as the spirit world took me clairvoyantly around the room. I saw, behind the door, a shelf. It was high up and was full of railway magazines. I got a feeling that it was high up because he did not want the boy (when he was little) touching the magazines and spoiling them. I was given the feeling by the spirit world that the boy was very disappointed that he wasn't allowed to play with the train or look at the magazines (clairsentience).

The uncle came forward and I saw the word 'SORRY' in front of my eyes. I then saw the magazines in a different attic and knew they had been kept by a member of the family.

It was a simple message that started off with an image of a Hornby train in an attic. By staying with the train and letting the spirit world direct me, the information expanded. It was like a story was being relayed. It was and is magical.

We do not need to search for the information, it is already there. The spirit world do not leave us when our energy dips, we lose sight, sense or a feeling of them. We come out of the power.

It took me years to understand what it meant when people talked about staying in the power. I remember thinking, where is this power? How do I find it? The power is the energy of the spirit world. It is blending with it and using the three senses (unconsciously because once you start being conscious of what sense you are using the energy will loosen) of seeing, feeling and hearing that enable a communication to take place or of being at one with the energy of the spirit world.

Giving a message when it is evidential in its detail can, as it did with me and my message from my niece through Sophie, change thinking. It stirs something within a heart and touches something within the soul. I like to say it ignites a spark within a person's being that once ignited, cannot be undone. That flame has been lit and it changes a person's life. For me, I had always felt something else but the message I was given, and it wasn't long, but a part of the message in its detail (one word) I knew that the spirit world without a shadow of a doubt existed.

Have you ever experienced such a message? How did it change your life?

When you believe that you do not die, you realise that everything you do is important. That you cannot live this one life you have and enjoy it as much as possible, come hell or high water. It means that you become aware of a higher power of something much bigger than we see with our physical eyes, that there is much more to this life than you can ever imagine and life takes on a different hue.

Chapter Thirteen

I quite often get emotional myself now when I give a reading. I feel the emotion of the sitter and the communicator. I have at times tried so hard to not cry and I will say at these times "Please excuse me, I am feeling a bit emotional myself!"

I am very conscious of body language and it is a very important to me as I am able to see the emotion behind the physical outward signs and also someone's words. I do not do it consciously but mixed with my past studies and work experience. I have had to handle some very tricky situations. It just happens.

Someone can sit there with their arms, legs, hands and everything else folded in an attempt to unconsciously shut themselves out, but I feel the emotion and quite often I am able to work with this and help them unravel themselves. It is easy to do this, but one of the best ways is with humour. From being wound around themselves like a tight corkscrew someone will just wilt. It is lovely to see and then I am happy.

It is easy to feel empathy with someone, especially when you have experienced the same as the person sitting in front of you. We have all experienced the death of a loved one. That is the biggest thing that I have in common with anyone who comes for a sitting. I really understand. I get emotional and when I do, I feel it in my heart and then I feel tears. This has not always been the case. I believe this is when I am really in a communication, as with Ben. I felt it, the whole room felt it and were in it with me. It was a communication from the heart and was filled with love, as was the room.

I feel it has a place and a time, as was the case that evening.

I am aware that this is sometimes my own emotion and sometimes, though not always, it is important to keep this in check. Empathy has a role, especially when a person is distraught. It would be completely useless if the medium is in shreds as well. This can be difficult as this is the whole thing about being a medium, having a heightened sensitivity, especially when we are working. We are open and feel more than the usual five senses. So being aware and keeping it in check is quite important.

I have already mentioned Barbara. She was at the Arthur Findlay College with me in 2016 and gave me a message from Ms Jones. I was delighted to have met her she showed me how important it is to keep emotions in check but still feel the information.

We paired up to work together. She went first to tune in and started to cry and then to sob. I sat there and thought, oh my goodness what is she picking up? I looked over at John Jonson who was busy and then looked back at Barbara "Are you ok?" Remember, I was supposed to be getting the message.

Then It was my turn. I reeled off all the information I was getting or seeing, as I am very Clairvoyant, and gave it to her. I did not feel it. I learnt to feel through my solar plexus that week and Barbara learnt to not feel quite so much. It is a balance. Being a clairvoyant robot is no good, neither is being over emotional.

So, we had two opposite people working together. One who felt every emotion past and present from every conceivable angle, and me the other end not feeling anything, just giving the information out. What a great opportunity to learn from each other and what a coincidence that we were put together.

Sometimes though, it does not matter what you say or do, you will find that there are people out there who will not take any information no matter what you say. I have known I am right as I am getting the information. This happened to me at a demonstration I did in a beautiful, very old pub. Unfortunately, it was quite noisy (so difficult). I did not go back and also told the organiser that it was not an ideal set up for communication with the spirit world unless it was for a ghost hunt (as the place was haunted).

I went to the young lady. "I believe you have just been promoted"
"yes"
"You work in health care"
"yes"
"I have a lady with me. She is your Nan." I then described her.
"No, I can't take that"
I then described this lady's house.
"no."
"You recall staying there?"
"no". I then gave her the message, "no". My energy was beginning to wane so I went back to the beginning.
"You understand the job change?"
"no"
"You work in healthcare?"
"no". I now began to get a bit annoyed as I was fully aware that this young lady was being difficult.

"Why you are here? I am going to leave you with the information I have given you, whether you can take it or not. Your Nan wishes you lots of love. Lots of love from me as well".

All of a sudden I got a picture of a red mini. "I am being shown a red mini. I believe you purchased one recently. It has an 'E' in the number plate and the number 6", (her Nan had not finished yet). She just stared at me looking embarrassed. So, it happens. Not very often but occasionally. The spirit world sort it out, or in this case, her Nan. She was also telling me she could be difficult, which is what the message was. I passed this on very tactfully.

I once asked the spirit world why some people had not stayed in my life (we have already talked about people coming in and going out of our lives and how this can be difficult sometimes). The answer came to me in a dream.

I saw someone I used to know. He was in a classroom with a group of people that were all in suits. They were all business men. They were in this class to learn, as we do when we sit in a normal physical class lessons.

I was in a different class. I knew that the lessons being taught were lessons for the growth of this person's soul within the environment he was in on the earth plane, that is why our lives had taken a different path. I did not need the same experiences for my own soul growth. So, we are here to progress in a spiritual sense and what a difficult school it is!

Can you recall going through a difficult time that gave you an understanding you did not have before?

Chapter Fourteen

I love churches. I have been in a few. Big cathedrals with the most amazing architecture and stained glass windows. I love them, they tell a story. The walls spill their history into the atmosphere of tales told from the past marriages, deaths, births, baptisms and then back again as new memories are created with the new people that walk into the church, bringing in one form or another the energy of love. There is a poem that I completely resonate with. It is written by George Herbert and is called 'The church floor'.

An Indian mystic (known as a Swami) was once asked, "Do you believe in God?" He said "I don't believe. I know I am god."

I recently went into my town to buy some material but the shop was closed as I was too early. I thought, I will go for a coffee. I saw a sign 'this way cakes and coffee' so I followed it and it took me up a path to a very old church.

I went in. I picked a piece of cake, walked along the table and asked for a coffee. Settling myself at a table looking at the windows, the pulpit and the christening font everything seemed very familiar having been brought up in the catholic faith, but the church had a different label, it was called the church of England. It had a sense of peace, a stillness that no matter how noisy it became it stayed there humming silently in the background.

I picked up a piece of paper advertising a service 'Come and find God'. I sat there getting more and more puzzled. What am I doing here?

Looking around at the people who were filling the tables, the lady on money duties got muddled up, I wondered if they came to church? Have they found God already? Do they look as if they had found God? What do you look like when you find God? And so it went on and then I thought, I think a lot of these people look as if they need to find God, hence the paper.

Then the answer came like a bolt of lightning. I realised that this was not a place where you find God, it is a place where you find God within yourself. God is not a God out there, we all have that same essence in our hearts and souls. The essence that connects each and every one of us is "love". When the Indian Mystic said he was God, he was right. We all are because we have the same essence.

I mentioned before the people in my young years; Maria, the rickshaw man and the goat lady. They didn't need to find God, they were so close to there own souls that they lived and breathed that love, that is why I was drawn to them. They were themselves, their authentic selves, as close to their own spirit as you can get because of their beliefs and simple lives. They showed me what love is. What pure spirit is. Perhaps the people in the church that day were so far removed from their own spirit that the energy of the place shows them love and brings them closer to their own soul, which is love. They are not finding God out there; they are connecting to themselves by the energy of church itself.

They are being touched by an energy that is universal that is within each and everyone of us that connects us all. That is a spiritual energy.

When I was a child I believed in God. I believed God was out there, up there, looking out for me. I believed that when it thundered it was God banging on a table because he was angry.

Now I do not believe in God. I believe in a creator and I believe that the creator is full of compassion, kindness and love. I believe we all have this energy at our core. It is a part of us and within us.

I believe there are different Gods, higher beings and angelic beings that are right on the periphery of our awareness and those beyond. Our pure authentic selves go back to the spirit world when our earthly lives or bodies die.

We do not die. I know, I have died. It is what set me off on this journey of ups and downs. It made my life difficult because I became aware and the majority of people are not aware.

The ones that label themselves as spiritual are quite often not because they are driven by ego and the personality and not by spirit. It does not matter how many courses you do or what qualifications you have. If you are not connected to your own soul and the feelings of others, you are not truly spiritual. Being connected to your own soul and the spirit world is being connected to love, compassion and kindness in everything you do.

It is hard being a spiritual person on the earth because we are in effect, shackled by a body, but we can be free to experience spirit if we so choose. If we choose or when we choose does not matter, we have all the time in the universe to do so. There is no rush.

And last but not least I would like to mention Karma and my understanding of it. It is the gentle loving flow of cause and effect. It is gentle and lovingly orchestrated by the spirit world. As I mentioned before, the reasons we are here and the lessons we have come to learn, every action has an effect on another person, including thoughts (everything is energetic in nature). We quite often do not know (whilst in the physical body) the true extent of the affect of our actions on another and with gentle loving synchronicities, we will experience the same. Sometimes we are hardly aware of it.

However, I believe when someone deliberately and consciously hurts another by words, thought or deed and they are trying to cause deliberate harm to another, this has a more karmic consequence. I believe (and have the chills as I write as the spirit world is very near), that they will experience directly the same, either in the same life time or another. They will have to go through the experience for them to gain an understanding of the consequence of their actions.

I believe this is the natural order of things and the universe and also a very important and significant universal law. That applies to all life, including our own spirits and souls.

So perhaps when we hear that saying 'put yourselves in my shoes' when you do or say anything to another because you will experience the same. After all, if you were aware of the consequence of doing something you would not have done it in the first place. Therefore, awareness and doing hurtful things do not go hand in hand.

When you believe in Karma you realize that every single one of us has a responsibility in the way we treat others.

I have given messages to family members who have stuck together because they are family and looking out for each other, even though some behaviours are not quite right. This is very admiral but from a spiritual perspective it is less so.

Bad behaviour is just that. It will have to be accounted for regardless of who it is. At the end of the day, we are ultimately responsible and accountable for ourselves and our actions. I know this because of my near death experience. I think that surely it would be better to mend things in this life time and erase the consequences of it than experience it personally in another or at a later date.

This is where love comes in, where being honest and open and truthful in all that we do is the most loving thing we can do for another.

As I look back over my journey so far, I am amazed at the synchronicities, the people who have played a major role in my life, the ones who, without a shadow of a doubt, were meant to be there. People who were not family members; Aunt Nell, Mike, Miss Jones. It perhaps makes me think that I have always been in the right place for these people to come in when they did.

But most of all this story is very similar to yours. It is full of amazing experiences. People who have come to support me when I needed it. To love me and those in my younger years who showed me what love was.

I talked at the beginning about love being the most important thing in life. Nothing else is more important and by writing this I have realised that I, like you, have been shown by many different people love in many forms along the way.

The Love shown to us is not always or just from family.

I believe my family members gave me the spring board with bag of tools and things to overcome (the loss of my mum) and the consequent search for love. Its meaning and the reason why we die and what death is or is not. They gave me some personality traits, both positive and negative, as tools to help me or otherwise in the growth of my own soul. The death of my mum enabled me to work in helping others to understand 'what death is not' by my work as a medium and healer.

We are all teachers and pupils and I keep being reminded of the book Celestine prophecies. Everyone you meet in every encounter has a message for you and you for them.

As I look back, I have been aware of a magical energy weaving its way in between all the ups, downs and flat moments in my life. This magical energy has been the spirit world. It is there all the time in all our lives, loving and guiding us through the mirage of our journey on the earth plane this time………….. until we go home x

An afterthought

My sister no longer eats worms, wears long skirts with Doc Martins or pinches my food. She now wears pink! Like me. She goes to Marks and Spencer's and colours her hair blonde. We have reached an understanding. She really does not care what I do, as long as I am ok. She no longer has Tinkerbell in a match box in her pocket, a shiny, sparkly spirit all of her own that she held so gently and perfectly in the palm of her hand so as not to hurt her in any way, that I knew she was real and who I was desperate to see but couldn't, because she wasn't for me she was for my sister. Now she just has the memory of her in her heart.
I understand our relationship and why we are here together thanks to Ann. Funny that but also wonderful

xx